Thoughts

Thoughts

- **On Apparitions**
- **Chastisements**
- **The Church**

By: William A. Reck

Published by:
The Riehle Foundation
P.O. Box 7
Milford, Ohio 45150

Published by: The Riehle Foundation
P.O. Box 7
Milford, OH 45150

For additional copies of this book address the Publisher.

ISBN: 1-877678-23-6

Library of Congress Catalog Card No.: 93-083447

TABLE OF CONTENTS

INTRODUCTION

The title of this book is *Thoughts*. Please accept it as such—the writer's thoughts on current apparitions, chastisement, and the Church of today.

The purpose is an "awareness." Hopefully, the end result will cause the reader to delve more deeply into the process of discernment. It seems to be something of which we are in need.

Reports of supernatural phenomena seem to be growing at an alarming pace today. With it comes a great interest in potential chastisement, given the rather pitiful condition of the present world. And then there is the rather divided and confusing status of the Church and its teachings. Additionally, these conditions certainly make for interesting reading. Vatican II is now thirty years old. We are then provided with several decades of results to measure, to analyze.

Musings on chastisement, rapture, and the end times have always been with us, even since the Bible, though today they admittedly seem more necessary for a just God. Examining the past helps us to be able to piece it all together. Such can be done with apparitions, for example, in a book called *The Final Hour*, by Michael

Brown. It links and summarizes the major apparitions of the past 150 years and the messages provided.

The primary need, then, might be one of discernment—a need to more carefully scrutinize the materials with which we are being bombarded, including those which come from this writer.

I also wish to state that, although I am a director of The Riehle Foundation, this publication offers only my own personal viewpoint. Although the book is being published by the foundation, it is not necessarily a position statement of the foundation. I apologize to those who may think my viewpoints are too strong or opinionated, or who do not appreciate my sometimes strange sense of humor. However, I probably won't change either one. Here then, are some THOUGHTS. You discern.

William A. Reck

PART I

APPARITIONS

As a teenager (and we won't go into how many years ago that was), I remember watching the movie versions of Lourdes and Fatima. That was the only information I had ever seen concerning something called "an apparition." It all seemed so distant, so mystical to me, like the Bible did. Boy have times changed. The Marian Movement is reaching a crescendo; claims of apparitions and heavenly messages are coming from everywhere giving both reasons for hope and predicted disasters. These are exciting times. It is the era of Our Lady as proclaimed by Pope John Paul II some six years ago when he announced the new "Marian Year." It seems like it was all in answer to Mary's diminished role that mistakenly resulted from Vatican II, and I say, "Alleluia!"

But is it all good? Or true? I verify that I have no authority in the discernment of apparitions, so you are simply reading one person's opinion. Recognize it as that.

On the other hand, my work through The Riehle Foundation during the past six years might provide some experience that could be useful. During this six year period it seems that most books and/or

1

manuscripts regarding any apparition or locution, anywhere in the world, has sooner or later found its way to our office. The volume today has become overwhelming, and at times, a little disturbing. What is happening?

Well, one possibility might be that it is all getting out of control. More frightening is the possibility that the evil one has become heavily involved. From what we have seen in the past 18 to 24 months, there are now many thousands of people involved with apparitions and messages everywhere around the world. During this period, it seems the United States has now become a focal point. Boy, have we seen an explosion in the number of apparitions and printed messages. Pretty exciting stuff. Reason for hope? Or for alarm? One thing is becoming evident. It seems there are less and less people who are taking the time to try to discern any of it.

Despite my lack of authority on this issue, I feel strongly that if Satan can't prevent this explosion of apparitions and messages, he surely can mess up some of them, or worse yet, create some of his own. The end result could discredit them all. There's really no sense in our doubting the existence of apparitions. If we do, I guess we have to throw out the Bible. Adam and Eve had the first one. God has always visited His people and today it seems like He is mostly sending His mother. Apparitions have always been there.

In June of 1981, six children reported seeing the Blessed Virgin Mary on a hillside in a remote village in Yugoslavia. The repercussions were to be felt around the world. Now, twelve years later, the summit of the experience has still not been reached. However, the events of that little, remote village of Medjugorje and the daily apparitions of Our Lady seemed to have ignited an explosion of supernatural manifestations the world has probably never experienced before.

Apparitions, visions, and heavenly messages are nothing new to the Catholic Church. They are nothing new to Christianity in general, or even to the Jewish people of the Old Testament. The Bible gives us a full complement of such occurrences from Moses to the Apostles. Prophets abound in the Scriptures. Even the Blessed Virgin Mary herself was the recipient of apparitions. Throughout the centuries, saints and doctors of the Church, the Hall of Fame of Church heroes, have left us their memoirs, teachings, diaries and literary works complete with testimonies of supernatural visits, visions and messages. Still, Medjugorje seems to have drawn us into a whole different scenario.

First of all, it needs to be stated that Medjugorje has probably produced more conversions than anything else the Church has seen in the last fifty years. More specifically, never since Vatican II, the aftermath of which has all but devastated the Catholic Church, have we witnessed such a profound return to the faith by such a multitude of people from every corner of the earth. Over 15,000,000 people have made that treacherous journey to that remote little village in a far off land, and probably twice as many more have been influenced by the events through the dozens and dozens of books and videos that have sprung up as a result. Devotion to the Blessed Virgin Mary is only a by-product. More importantly, we have witnessed a tremendous return to the Rosary, a new birth in prayer groups and other Marian organizations. Hundreds of thousands have suddenly returned to the Sacraments. Daily Mass and monthly confession have been added to a menu that includes daily prayer and fasting one or two days a week. In a Church, and in a world that has a hard time even defining sin anymore or recognizing that Satan exists, it is refreshing indeed to see so many people who are proud to wear their faith on their sleeve and proclaim it to all they meet. Praise God! It certainly does appear that the Holy Spirit, perhaps through His spouse, the Blessed Virgin Mary, renews the Church by revitalizing the laity when the ordained Church seem to be having particular difficulties.

With that said, we need to recognize the existence of the other side of the coin. It is the darker side, the one wrought with problems and the difficulties of discernment; for you see, the past twenty years has given birth to a great explosion of supernatural manifestations. It has become particularly prevalent in the United States. As of this writing, there are over 30 reported visionaries in 15 different states. Supernatural messages seem to be coming from everywhere.

It is very apparent that modern day technology has played a major role in this crescendo of apparitions and locutions. The recognized apparitions at LaSalette, Lourdes and Fatima did not include any TV cameras or video recorders. There were no technical devices to test, to measure, to evaluate reactions of visionaries. There was no air travel, no mass communication network. Believe it or not, there wasn't even a fax machine. Medjugorje has opened a whole new concept of connecting the average person, anywhere in the world, with the messages and testimonies of visionaries anywhere in the world. In addition to the printed word in books and the visual support provided through video reproduction, newsletters, magazines and newspapers provide update information to literally millions of people.

In the first instance, this isn't all bad. It has been a positive inspiration to countless souls. There is little doubt that Bernadette would have welcomed such innovations at Lourdes in 1858. It probably would have eliminated a lot of difficulty, mistrust, and unbelief she was forced to endure. In any event, Medjugorje evidently became a springboard for a wave of new claimed apparitions the world over. It even gave new life to apparitions that had begun prior to the Medjugorje event of 1981, or that had not been exposed to the world at large for one reason or another previously. As such, the apparitions at Akita (Japan), Betania (Venezuela), Cairo (Egypt), Cua (Nicaragua), Kibeho (Africa), for example, suddenly blossomed, not to mention events that had taken place in many locations in Europe behind the iron curtain. There appeared to be strong evidence that the world had been receiving some heavenly injections to offset the disease of sin. Just as important as the disclosure of these claimed apparitions was the new found knowledge that most contained similar messages. It has become undeniable that our Creator and the Mother of Jesus are trying very desperately to get our attention.

But this book is not about witnessing to this myriad of apparitions that have enveloped our world during these past two decades. There are other books available that cover that issue in depth. In contrast, this book is an attempt to merely call attention to a most serious need, the result of this wave of claimed apparitions, and this need is discernment. With the speed of modern technology, coupled with natural human curiosity and excitement over paranormal activity, rapid dissemination of information can take precedence over accuracy, wisdom or church sanctions. It not only can produce false information, but can give Satan many opportunities to tamper. Could it be that we elevate the importance of these reported messages to the possible detriment of the Church and the faith of the people involved? As one rather upset person once told me: "This whole thing is starting to become a group of apparition chasers. They just run from one to the next—wherever it is." That may be stretching the point just a bit, but it is worth noting.

If we truly believe that we are being visited by the Blessed Virgin Mary and her Divine Son, Our Lord and Savior Jesus Christ, then we must also believe that the power of evil also exists and that he comes also, to disrupt, to confuse, to divide, to deceive. Since the existence of Hell and the existence of Satan is mentioned hundreds of times in the Bible, I guess I better believe that both exist. Thus the need to see if he fits in here anywhere, the need to discern. In expanding on this, I wish to first state the following:

> I have no intent to try to validate or disapprove any apparition or to discredit any claimed visionary. That is not within my power and would be detrimental to all. I am not in that privileged group of seers or locutionists, so who am I to say which is, or which is not, authentic. It is merely my intent to present some facts, or claimed facts, that give evidence to the great need for discernment in this apparent period of numerous heavenly visitations.

The next step then, the big one, is the process of trying to determine whether all these new apparition claims are truly authentic. Should we follow them? Or not? Is Satan duping us? Are some merely an overactive imagination? Someone caught up in the euphoria of all this—well meaning though it may be? I don't know! Do you? One thing seems evident, and that is that there may be a need to question more, and accept less on face value.

One of the more obvious signs that Satan truly is involved in a big way in all of this is any confusion, dissension, even confrontation that exists among the visionaries and apparition sites worldwide. Periods of the "spiritual dark night" also become common with many of the seers involved. Messages of despair, chastisement, and the wrath of God have become commonplace. Others might give evidence of falling outside of accepted Catholic Doctrine, or at least borderline, and some might be in contrast to Scripture. Satan does appear to be present, hidden under a supposed veil of goodness and light as he usually is.

I have often reproached the Lord: "Lord, PLEASE, consult with me first before you do all these things so that I know what is going on and I don't have to sit here like a dummy." But He doesn't listen to me and just goes right on as if He is still in charge of the whole universe or something. So here I sit like a dummy. But it appears there are many of us in the same boat, so I have the feeling that I am not the only one who has suddenly become very alarmed at all of these apparitions and messages, especially the reported increase of events in the United States.

Personally, I can't seem to handle the volume, or to keep up with all of them. Have you ever found yourself sort of pulled off of one prayer project from a certain apparition message, because you were suddenly encouraged to begin this or that program coming from another source? Speaking just for myself, I have enough difficulty keeping abreast of all the materials and messages that our own apostolate has published over the past five years dealing with Mary's visits to her children of the world.

In sorting through all of these many volumes of messages, prayers, extra rosaries for this, more chaplets for that, "Jesus said to read this book or that book," go to this conference or that apparition site, I am suddenly aware that one can come up with a 27 hour day. On the other hand, maybe all my past sins require a 27 hour day of prayer and reparation, but, really, I don't think that's part of the game plan. Regardless, discernment might be something we really should start to look at. There is a lot of reference in the Bible that we can check out—both for and against private revelation.

Take care not to be misled. Many will come in my name saying "I am he and the time is at hand." Neither must you be perturbed when you hear of wars and insurrections. These things are bound to happen first, but the end does not follow immediately. (*Luke* 21:8-9).

If anyone tells you at that time, "Look the Messiah is here, or He is there," do not believe it. False messiahs and false prophets will appear, performing signs and wonders so great as to mislead even the chosen. (*Matt.* 24:23-25).

Do not stifle the Spirit. Do not despise prophecies. Test everything; retain what is good. (*1 Thess.* 5:19-21).

The Bible tells us that there has been and will be visions and that old men will prophesy and young men will dream dreams. Peter tells us (2 *Peter*, Chapter 2), about false teachers, past and future. Prophets and visions abound in Scripture. And, all of them weren't right either. Does that invalidate the Bible? Then why should it invalidate any current claimed visionary in America, or wherever. I believe St. Paul and the Apostles provided many references about the "return of the Lord" in their lifetime. They missed by almost two thousand years—so far. Jonas also preached the certain destruction of Ninive after forty days. It wasn't. Some very famous saints, doctors of the Church, also made some errors regarding their prophecies or heavenly messages. Does this then exonerate all current claimed visionaries, or does it just throw more doubt on all? Personally, I am pleased that I don't know the answer to that. It eliminates the possibility that I am qualfied to judge. But it does not eliminate the possibility (or the responsibility) that we all have to question, to discern.

Following are some excerpts from messages originating from visionaries/locutionists, all in the United States. They are from messages received by the visionary, or concern the particular apparition site. There is no intent here to identify any messenger, or to quote complete messages. Space wouldn't allow us to cover them all. This then, is merely an attempt to present some specific aspect or item for the purpose of showing a need for the reader's discernment.

— *My Mother, part of the Holy Trinity of God.* (Fourth person of the Trinity?)

— *I do not appear like this anywhere else on earth. No where are my graces being poured forth like they are here.*

— *Pope John Paul will be gone before 1993.*

— *The devil cannot read your thoughts.* (But to another visionary Our Lord apparently said: *Beware, the devil may get into your thoughts.*)

— *The pilgrims see angels appear here and also Mary.*

— *Here will I grant many healings. The blind will see, the deaf will hear, the lame will walk. Cancer and other ailments will be cured.*

— *You are to wear a new special medal which will allow you to identify Our Lord when he comes. . . Satan will also make a duplicate one.*

— *You are to write in the name of "Jesus Christ" on the election ballot.*

— *Children, if you do not believe this* (the messages), *then you stand accused before me.*

— At one site Jesus sometimes comes with what seems like a comedy routine.

— *All religions and priests and ministers are the same.*

— *These messages are to be added to revelation.*

— *Those who reject you* (the visionary), *reject me. All will be held accountable.*

— Some messages include specific details on the publishing of the messages—size of the book, style, layout, etc.

— Some messages include specific instructions to read certain books—("POEM OF THE MAN GOD," "MYSTICAL CITY OF GOD"), and recommendations on acquiring certain other books.

— Many messages from various locations also include specific references to third parties by name. The visionary is requested to send certain materials to this identified priest, to Mother Angelica, to that publisher, or to have so and so do this or write that. Future situations regarding other persons are presented. Other persons are brought into the events as part of the overall responsibility. One even had a message for President Bush.

St. Teresa of Avila, a Doctor of the Church, has left us volumes on the spiritual life. Included is much data on private revelations and apparitions. Among these admonishments she had this to say: "Speaking of locutions, if they treat of some weighty matter in which we are called to act, or if they concern any third person, we should consult some confessor who is both learned and a servant of God before attempting or thinking of acting on them, even though we may feel more and more convinced of their truth and of their divine origin."

Some of the messages being circulated around the United States seem to be opposed to each other. There seem to be messages coming from Our Lord or Our Lady which warn of other claimed locutionists, but never of the one being spoken to:

— (Jesus) *Some people are hearing messages in their heads but it is illusion.*

— *Questions are being asked of one another. Answers are being given to one another. Man thinks he has everything figured out. He thinks he can foresee the future and its happenings. Woe to the man who jumps ahead of me.*

— *False prophets destroy what I have built by their promises.*

— (Jesus, regarding prophecies from others): *You do not need to read them.* (Our Lady): *There are many false messages. They are not coming from God. I am the Blessed Virgin Mary.*

— *Keep guard over your minds and tongues. These are powerful tools that the evil one uses. By means of them, he whispers his lies, and the uttered words cause divisions and grave harm...Do not rely heavily upon your human opinions in any matter. Where human thought and human feeling are called upon, the evil one divides, confuses and arouses the lower base passions...Rely upon no man, no government.* (Does that say don't discern anything, just accept it? Or just accept what a visionary says?)

— *Woe to those who persecute my little ones, seeking by every clever word of human origin to refute the Divine Wisdom which God imparts to His chosen ones.*

Yet the same visionaries all have imaginative and intellectual visions, audible voices and interior locutions. Regarding the "hearing messages in their heads" quoted above, the same visionary hears a voice speaking to him/her, sometimes words implanted in his/her mind. Additionally, other persons are brought into the event and are given responsibilities and then also receive locutions.

I wonder if anyone gets the feeling that some messages are being presented as being more important than the words of Scripture? There also seems to be a need to read between the lines on some of those messages that appear like Our Lady is admonishing anyone who would doubt any of her alleged messengers. We have seen this on a worldwide basis, where you can interpret the message as saying "you better believe this or else" and that other claimed visionaries are false and only so-and-so is the true one. Didn't we read somewhere, "test everything?"

— *You have a best-seller here* (Jesus to one visionary regarding the planned message book).

— *Mankind shall receive no further mercy or warning.*

— *Mercy is everlasting when it comes from the Father.*

— *Soon my Father's mercy will end.*

The subject of mercy seems to be kind of, on again-off again, through a number of messages. In one message it is as the Jesus of the Gospels, mercy personified. In another message it seems like He cancelled it all.

— One site has been invited to provide a healing spring by tapping into an existing water line.

— Jesus has stated at one site that to postpone the chastisement, people must come here.

— At several sites, Jesus and Our Lady appear to be at the beckoned call of the visionary, at any time, along with an assortment of saints. At another site a visionary has apparitions for hours on end and even saw Our Lady appear with a tambourine doing the Mexican hat dance.

— At a number of sites, humility seems to be a major criteria, which certainly appears to be a positive attribute, but at other times it includes threats, the identification of other people, and the immediate need for books, videos, medals, and prayers to be produced.

TRUE OR FALSE:

Is it or isn't it? I for one don't know. I would prefer that it all be authentic and although I am sure some have been given the gift of discernment, for most of us it is a very elusive gift. I am sometimes amazed at the stack of material in my office regarding apparitions and messages. It is a couple of feet high. Jesus had it all covered though (as He always does), when

He said, *You shall know the tree by its fruits.* Whoops! Jesus, I have a question, "Does 'fruits' mean the message, the messenger, or the acceptance by the people?"

In the *Acts of the Apostles* (5:38-39), the legal expert Gamaliel had this to say to the Sanhedrin as they pondered how to get rid of the Apostles: *My advice is that you have nothing to do with these men. Let them alone. If their purpose or activity is human in its origins, it will destroy itself. If, on the other hand, it comes from God, you will not be able to destroy them without fighting God himself.* That seems fair enough.

Still, that does not eliminate our own individual need for discernment. It is not only our right, it is an obligation. And I believe the rationale we have all heard many times, as stated above, is the passage that says, "You shall know the tree by its fruits." (Message, messenger and the good fruits of the faithful.) Our Lord tells us that Satan cannot produce good fruits. But I wonder if he can produce good fruits, say for just two years, and then have the whole thing come crashing down to the despair of many good people? I think he can. He's been doing it for centuries. I remember seeing an account of Magdalen of the Cross, a Franciscan Nun of the XVI century, who early on had given herself to the devil. He promised her much. She entered the convent at age seventeen and was three times Abbess of her monastery. Aided by the demon, she simulated all the mystical phenomena of ecstasy, levitation, stigmata, revelations and prophecies repeatedly fulfilled. At the point where she believed she was near death, she confessed it all and was exorcised.

I believe the claimed apparitions at Necedah and Bayside have been rejected by the Church. Still, there are many who believe in them due to the signs and wonders they have witnessed there. Many came to pray in fervent devotion to Our Lady and in adoration to her Divine Son. The sun spun, there were great "light shows" and of course, many rosaries turned gold. But whose light was it?

"Test everything," Scripture tells us. I do not believe Our Lord or Our Lady come to earth to be book critics. I don't believe they want you to run out and buy $35.00 books, or even recommend them. I also wonder if they really give you a recommended reading list, like a "Religion 101" class. I have problems believing they come to joke around or that they come to threaten, intimidate, promote an apparition site, or get you involved in anything other than your own spiritual well-being. Given the fact that Our Lord has stated: *You know not the day or the hour* of His coming, I have difficulty accepting the fact that anyone is receiving the layout for the chastisement of the world in complete detail and time frame. I do believe they are making appearances as never before and that Our Lady most certainly is making an urgent plea to all of her children of the world. I do believe they are appearing to many persons in the United States. I do not believe there is an immediate need to publish a book on every apparition or to spread the message of every apparition or locution to the population in general. Boy, would that make a high stack.

One visionary claims the ability to bilocate, has the gift of instant healing and can foretell the future. Another stresses unity and states the "World Council of Churches" will be the force that creates it.

Some people have a problem with the vast array of "code names" popping up with claimed visionaries:

"Spring Flower, "Thornbush," "Little Pebble," "Hidden Flower," "The Trumpeter," "Little Flower," "White Dove," "Bluebird," "Little Dove," etc. Is that questionable? Perhaps so. (Maybe not.) If the Lord gave me one, it might be, "My Big Turkey."

There also appears to be a problem with many prophecies that didn't materialize as scheduled. This was especially true concerning natural disasters, such as earthquakes. Sometimes this is explained away as "being delayed because of the volume of prayers." (Such was the case of a prediction of an earthquake that didn't happen in California.) This apparently means that a visionary giving prophecy can never be wrong—it can always be delayed or mitigated because of our responses. But that becomes harder to understand when you read a whole list of different messages by different messengers that emphatically state that the apostasy, the chastisement, the end times, the three days of darkness, the whole thing is coming down right now—now is the time—His hand cannot be stayed, and the reason for it all is your total lack of prayer and commitment. Then comes a message that says it has all been held back because of your prayer. Is Our Lord saying, "Hey, I was only kidding"?

Interestingly enough, I recall reading from an article in a rather old book outlining the position of some of the early doctors of the Church and their views of private revelation. Now I can't seem to locate the article to quote from, but I think the saint involved might be St. Thomas. In any case, this particular view did indeed claim that God often times creates these types of revelations just to scare His creatures. It's sort of a, "If I can scare 'em bad enough, maybe they'll start to pay attention to me." That may not be a bad idea, but somehow it just doesn't seem to fit.

With some visionaries there is a deep sense of humility and a desire to remain anonymous. They disdain publicity and shy away from the sensational. Others actively promote and feel a need to have their messages spread far and wide. Does that make a difference? Which is right? And is it a divine request, or a human decision?

There also seems to be a great amount of emphasis placed on "signs." What about all that phenomena that apparently surrounds these sites? Isn't that proof? It may well be—or maybe not. Doesn't the name "Lucifer" indicate an angel of light? Doesn't it say in the Bible that he will come as a false angel of light? Christine Gallagher is a highly thought of visionary from Ireland. She also claims many experiences and battles with Satan. Christine states that the greatest "light shows" she has seen have been put on by the devil. If Satan has such incredible powers to deceive and to destroy, to work miracles, to even take the Lord to the top of a mountain where he showed Him all the kingdoms of the world, can he turn a rosary golden color? If he can come as the Blessed Virgin Mary (attested to by many of the saints), can he create an image? St. Catherine had visions and apparitions for many years. Feeling herself favored with great graces, she had said audaciously to the devil: "Know that you could send me no temptation without my perceiving it" After this imprudent challenge, she had false apparitions of Our Lord and the Blessed Virgin Mary for five years (from the book, REVELATIONS—HOW TO JUDGE THEM, page 371).

The number of photos currently being passed around, the world over, is frightening. We have seen one picture which is claimed to have come from four different apparition sites as being "an authentic picture taken by so-and-so at such-and-such a place." The reproduction of the copies get worse and worse the farther it travels. Polaroid photos are the most popular and convey all kinds of images, particularly if taken into the sun or a strong light. All kinds of images are present if you turn it this way or that way or look at it from a certain angle. Fortunately (or unfortunately), I rarely see anything. (Maybe the Lord truly does think I'm a turkey.) On the other hand, there are specific photos that are quite dramatic, and unexplainable. It is hard to doubt their authenticity. Like many other articles associated with apparitions or sites, pictures quickly find their way to the marketplace. Regardless, the Church will never approve or authenticate any apparition based on pictures, but it may be the reason to condemn some.

At The Riehle Foundation, we have evaluated over fifty manuscripts during the past three years that the foundation had decided not to publish. These manuscripts often involved some direct supernatural manifestation, or at least something similar emanating from a pilgrimage, usually to Medjugorje. It was not a case of not believing the content or the story, but simply answering my own question, "How many apparition books can we do?" At some point in time, I guess we all wonder whether the world really needs another visionary or message, or, do we just really need to start sorting out the ones we already have. On the other hand, Our Lord, and His Mother, evidently feel it is necessary to continue their messages to this troubled world.

On July 4, 1986, at six o'clock in the morning, I climbed Cross Mountain in Medjugorje. Once at the summit, my entire life changed in a heartbeat and I knew why I went there. I have seen the phenomenon of Medjugorje, so who am I to doubt anyone else. Furthermore, that experience turned my entire life and work over to the Blessed Virgin Mary and since then, I have witnessed unexplainable occurrences in Milford, Ohio, as well—both good and bad, both from good spirits and evil ones. Therefore it is impossible for me not to strongly believe that this indeed is the time of supernatural manifestations and that some very important Person is trying to get our attention. But, if I believe that, then I also have to believe the adversary is also, and there is a strong need to try to discern the difference. It is not a question of doubting the sometimes heroic efforts of people who claim to be simply messengers of the Lord; it is the need to make sure evil spirits are not deluding us.

Undeniable things are happening. A merciful God is calling to His people. Conversions abound and we have all seen renewal take place in the hearts of so many. But the bad guy hasn't given up yet. The Bible tells us to keep oil in our lamps and keep them lit. It also tells us to remain awake and to recognize that *Satan is prowling about the world like a lion ready to devour souls.* Test everything! Discern! Your rosary turning gold, or a photo, will never prove an apparition or authenticate a visionary. Neither will a light you see, unless you can verify whose light it is. There is a great need to evaluate every message, for none of them will replace the Bible.

In the past several weeks, I have spent some time speaking with Gianna Talone from Scottsdale, Arizona.

It was Gianna who provided the lessons and messages contained in the books, I AM YOUR JESUS OF MERCY. I asked Gianna her opinion on the great influx of new visionaries, locutionists and messages that are spreading like wildfire throughout the world—whether she had any concerns.

To her credit Gianna stated that prudence is so necessary because of the element of human intrepretation entering into the messages. She stated that early on in her apparitions there may have been a possibility that what she perceived in a message was not what she actually conveyed. She stressed the complete need for humility and conformity to the word of God and stated that, "if I made any mistake, it was probably that I felt I knew so much early on in my experiences. Now, each day I can tell you that I realize I know nothing. I can see now that Our Lord gave me certain tests and allowed Satan to try to tempt or confuse me in my thinking. It is also very easy to be mis-understood or mis-quoted, or to place too much emphasis on your own human interpretation. Caution needs to be exercised right now because if Satan wants to deceive people, it can be through the influx of false messages, masking those that are authentic. An element of fear is surfacing."

It is very refreshing to hear someone who apparently has lived these very difficult experiences stress the need for humility and conformity to the will of God. It is good to recognize that visionaries are only human beings, just like you and me, and to have a visionary express caution about chasing apparitions or putting too much emphasis on whatever a visionary says. I appreciate hearing of the pitfalls from someone who has apparently been there. Regardless, it still sounds like good advice.

PART II

CHASTISEMENT

Much of the material attributed to current visionaries deals with chastisement. It appears to be having a rather dramatic effect on the people following it. Is this good? Or bad?

Unless we are living in a cave somewhere, far away from the evils of our current world, we do not need any visionary to tell us that the world is in big trouble. And if we truly believe in God, in Jesus Christ as our Lord and Savior, in the tenets of our faith, and in the Blessed Virgin Mary as the Mother of God, then we have to ask ourselves: "How long can God let all of this go on?" You sorta think that the world deserves whatever it gets. There is no need to address all the evils of the world here, we are all aware of them. The sin and failure of mankind covers all aspects of creation, from the environment, society, the family, to the individual, and includes the Church. Where does a just God draw the line?

Many of the messages being presented to us by visionaries today seem to answer that question, and in vivid detail. The problem once again is discernment. It is probably prudent to again note here that I do not have the stamp of approval for any of it, nor am I in a position to disapprove. But, there is a responsibility on the part of all of us to evaluate and question.

In reading Scripture it sometimes seems like most of the Old Testament was steeped in chastisement. There were all kinds of prophets bringing news to the people, and most of it bad. Was the world before Christ as bad as it is now? That's hard to imagine. In any case, it seems like a just God was laying some heavy hits on his people throughout. There is some heavy suffering going on as recorded in the books of the Old Testament. The emergence of the Incarnation of the Word, the Messiah, seemed to change all that for a while and the "Good News" was that of love, humility, hope, and redemption. But even the Lord laid out some bad news as well:

> *Nation will rise against nation, one kingdom against another. There will be famine and pestilence and earthquakes in diverse places.* (*Matt.* 24:7-8).

> *Many will falter then, betraying and hating one another. False prophets will rise in great numbers to mislead many. Because of the increase of evil, the love of most will grow cold.* (*Matt.* 24:10-14).

> *There will be signs in the sun, the moon and the stars. On the earth, nations will be in anguish, distraught at the roaring of the sea and the waves. Men will die of fright in anticipation of what is coming upon the earth. The powers in the heavens will be shaken. After that, men will see the Son of Man coming on a cloud with great power and glory.* (*Luke* 21:25-27).

Those are some pretty heavy words and sure fit where we are and what we might need right now. Other prophets picked it up from there and presented us with additional insight into this realm of chastisement. And unfortunately, not all were very accurate and this includes some of the big names from the "Hall of Fame" of the Catholic Church. The Apostles themselves thought it was all to occur in their lifetime.

What are some of the current visionaries saying, in the United States in particular? Again, there is no intent here to identify any visionary by name, or even question their source or their intent. It is simply a case of providing some excerpts from existing messages to identify a possible need for discernment on the part of those reading them. They are presented as messages from Our Lord or Our Lady and a selection is as follows:

— *We are in the last hours. . .the earthquake on the West coast will be devastating.* (Aug. '92).

— *The last three months of 1992 will be the total destruction of America. The land shall be ravaged.*

— *The earth will split in half.*

— *The great earthquake is not even months away.* (May '92).

— *A great war is coming. A great punishment is coming for California.*

— *Never has your continent seen such destruction. It will be worse than the civil war.* (May '92).

— *Pray intensely through the night, this is the last night you have. . .the hour has come. . .no more can be done.* (May '92).

— *Sell your stocks, put away your investments. . . Money is worthless. . .every hour should be spent in prayer.*

— *Antichrist has come. . .he wears human form and convinces all to whom he speaks. . .He is not born of woman. . .I have shown you the face of Antichrist.*

— *I solemnly tell you, the moment of great darkness has come.* (July '91).

— *At Bayside I have given you these warnings. And at Necedah I have given you these warnings. Now at this time throughout this world I give you this warning America.*

— *The time is not far away, my children. It is less than two years when he* (the Pope) *shall flee Rome only to return again to meet and embrace martyrdom for Holy Mother Church. Very soon will be seen in the nations of Italy, Spain, and France, rivalry within the streets, great social and political unrest.* (Given in 1990).

— *I tell you the conflict in the Persian Gulf shall not be short. . .Many nations shall wage war. From the smoke of this war shall rise the antichrist. He is here.* (Jan. '91).

— *The economy of the world shall collapse in a very short time.* (Jan. '91).

— *I do solemnly tell you that in the following months of this year* (Aug. '92) *you shall experience many signs which shall lead your world into total collapse. Tremendous earthquakes shall devastate, particularly in this country. . .the economy will collapse . . .the land shall be ravaged.*

— *The martyrdom of Pope John Paul II is imminent.* (June '92).

— *The time for the great schism is here.* (May '91).

— *Pray for the Pope who will soon be silenced.* (Jan. '91).

— *War will come, brutal, swift, changing the earth forever...attempts made to bring peace to the Persian Gulf are maneuvers by Satan's legions...the antichrist walks the earth and has come to a position of great power...Satan's legions will strike out even silencing the holy voice of the Vicar of Christ...chaos shall reign.*

In May of 1992 there seemed to be great concern over the chastisement, particularly in the form of an earthquake, all of which was to happen in California in June. These predictions included great detail of suffering and destruction and some rather strange methods and means of cures, and being physically saved.

Some of the messages of chastisement also seemed to include differences as to God's mercy and whether it was available to us or not:

— *There will be no more warnings...Man is not deserving of any more warnings.*

— *All will be given much warning before this happens.*

— *No more can my Father be merciful.*

— *He continues to pour His mercy onto mankind because of His endless love.*

— (Additional predictions for the major California earthquake called for it to happen in October of 1992.)

— *Do not let anyone tell you that this war will be over and peace will reign.* (Persian Gulf). *It is the chastise-*

*ment...This war shall spread to other lands...
Terrorism shall be the rule soon and no one shall be
safe. Life as it has been lived in this century shall
pass away.* (Jan. '91).

A number of messages over the past two years give
much detail regarding abortion being the reason to
trigger the chastisement. There are also many messages alluding to the great schism in the Church and
the imminent state of apostasy. Several messages stated
the prediction of the end of the Persian Gulf war, as
given by Our Lord.

Hey, that is a whole bunch of bad news and enough
to get your attention. It sure gets mine. Still, it would
seem that much of this information was common
knowledge in that is has been before us for some time.
The evil of abortion has been with us for twenty years
and few doubt that it calls out for vengeance from the
Lord. The Church is in somewhat of a shambles and
for those of us who have been involved, it is not difficult to see the creation of the "American Catholic
Church" perhaps being just around the corner. Those
two points alone are enough reason for the chastisement to come and I for one, think it will. But when?

Predicting the end of the Persian Gulf war didn't
require any visionaries. Anyone with a television set,
anywhere in the world, who watched the first war ever
fought and reported via television could have predicted
the end within a few days. Are all the above prophecies
wrong? Are some of them? Who am I to say. Didn't St.
Peter tell us that God is not on the same calendar or
time that we are:

> *In the Lord's eyes, one day is as a thousand
> years and a thousand years are as a day. The*

Lord does not delay in keeping his promise—though some consider it delay. Rather he shows you generous patience, since he wants none to perish but all to come to repentance. The day of the Lord will come like a thief... (2 Peter 3:8-10).

That seems to indicate that you can't rule out prophecy based only on our calendar as being the determination of whether we hit it or whether we missed it. Still, it's a good reason to stop and take a look at it. And there is a question of whether all this conjecture over the end times and chastisement is really worth the effort. I kind of think that it isn't. As HE said, *You know not the day or the hour.* Besides, what are you going to do about it? Is some of this our morbid curiosity playing tricks on us? Or, worse yet, Satan? If a certain predicted prophecy doesn't materialize, does that invalidate the messenger? I don't think so. It is simply another example of our need for discernment.

In my case, I can learn a lot from my wife. Aside from being a very spiritual lady, Fran is battling for her life against cancer. In the process, she has already consecrated her life to the Immaculate Heart of Mary and devotes all of her energies to working in Our Lady's ministry. If she knew the day of the coming chastisement, what would she do different in her life to prepare for it? The answer: nothing! Maybe that should be everybody's answer.

I really don't believe I have to prepare by wearing a certain medal, praying extra chaplets and rosaries for a dozen different causes, or spend so many minutes doing this or so many hours devoted to that. I don't think I'm supposed to be storing food and water or selling all my assets, or go out and buy a farm somewhere in the middle of no place. I really don't think you can outfox the Lord. If I do all that, and if He is really going to send a comet to strike and destroy the earth, He will probably make the center of impact right on my property. So much for that theory. Didn't HE spell all that out as well?

For whoever wishes to save his life will lose it, but whoever loses his life for my sake and that of the gospel will save it. (Mark 8:35).

It was interesting to read, a few months ago, of the church in Korea that had a special insight of the coming rapture and end times, and on a given date the congregation sold all of their property, quit their jobs and marched out to the countryside to await the event. Then, when the heavenly bus didn't come by, the community was left with all these unemployed and homeless people. Are some of us also waiting for a bus?

Billions, literally billions of people have lived on this earth prior to you and me. Do you know how many made it out of this world alive? That's right, so I guess the bottom line is that you and I are going to die. Ultimately, it really doesn't matter how, or when, or where. The only thing that is important is the condition of our souls. So that is the only thing we need to be concerned about. The rest of it is out of our hands— and everybody else's. Only HE has the answer. Speaking just for myself, I find much more hope in the messages from Medjugorje, or perhaps the "I AM YOUR JESUS OF MERCY" books. Our Lady's messages at Medjugorje truly seem to touch us where we really live and give hope and meaning and substance to the travails of our daily lives and the needs of our families. In fact, she warns us not to pursue the thoughts of war and chastisement, but says the only real need is for us to return to her Son. She, as was the case with her Son, comes to bring hope, not despair.

HOW ABOUT THE SAINTS?

What did the saints and Doctors of the Church have to say about all this apparition business? What has the past taught us? Michael Brown is as involved as anyone I know regarding the study of apparitions. He sent me sections of certain books on mystical theology that detail the thoughts and teachings of some of the more recognized names in Church annals regarding such phenomena.

Here are some tidbits:

St. Teresa of Avila and St. John of the Cross have some very negative things to say regarding apparitions. St. John stated: "These things are not necessary means to the divine union and at times are rather obstacles, owing to our evil tendencies. Desire for revelations deprives faith of its purity, develops a dangerous curiosity which becomes a source of illusions, fills the mind with vain fancies, and often proves the want of humility and of submission to Our Lord who has already given us all that is needed for salvation." He also speaks harshly of spiritual directors who push the seers forward attaching more importance to these visions and falsely building up the person in the process. He states, "Some directors bid the person to pray to God to reveal to them such and such things concerning themselves or others."

St. Teresa, speaking of visionaries, states: "It happens that some of them are of so weak an imagination, that whatever they think upon, they say they see it clearly, as it indeed seems to them; they also have so vigorous an understanding that they become quite certain of everything in their imagination."

St. John of the Cross further adds: "The devil rejoices greatly when a soul seeks after revelations and is ready to accept them; for such conduct furnishes him with many opportunities of delusions." St. Teresa adds: "When anyone can contemplate the sight of Our Lord for a long period of time, I do not believe it is a vision, but rather some overmastering idea." These two saints provide us with literally volumes of teachings on mystical theology, and, they are obviously very hard on visionaries. With that said, let us recognize that they also were visionaries. Does that mean that they disqualify themselves?

St. Ignatius, in his "Rules for the Discernment of Spirits" states: "It is the part of the devil to transform himself into an angel of light to enter at the outset into the pious desires of the soul, and to end by suggesting his own designs. Thus when he sees a soul given to the practice of virtue, he firsts suggests sentiments in harmony with that soul's good dispositions." He adds, "As soon as the devil sees us to be humble, he strives to inspire us with a false humility, that is to say, an excessive vicious humility." St. Teresa adds to that by saying, "The devil frequently fills our thoughts with great schemes, so that instead of putting our hand to what work we can do to serve our Lord, we may rest satisfied with working to perform impossibilities." (On the other hand, we are told that nothing is impossible with God!)

Let's add to all of that the knowledge that some of our most recognized saints have been prone to error in their teachings and literary works.

— St. Joan of Arc believed she would be saved by Our Lord from being burnt at the stake.

— St. Norbert affirmed that he knew through revelation that the Antichrist would come in his generation (XII century).

— St. Vincent Ferrer spent the last twenty-one years of his life announcing that the Last Judgment was at hand. He was certain of the truth of it through a vision, and through many miracles he performed. (Year 1400).

— The revelations of St. Bridget, St. Gertrude, and St. Catherine of Siena contradict each other.

— Catherine Emmerich, Mary of Agreda, St. Elizabeth of Schoenau, and St. Bridget all contradict each other as to when the Blessed Virgin Mary died.

— St. Bridget and Mary of Agreda ("MYSTICAL CITY") contradict each other with regard to the Nativity at Bethlehem.

— St. Colette said she had a vision indicating that St. Anne had been married three times.

— Historians and theologians have discovered many errors in the works of Blessed Anna Maria Taigi.

— A number of errors had been attributed to Mary of Agreda, to the extent that Clement XIV forbade her beatification in 1771.

— St. Catherine of Siena thought she had a vision where Our Lady stated that she was not immaculate.

— Catherine Emmerich had a symbolic vision showing that Mary of Agreda's works had been altered.

— Pope Leo X published a Bull prohibiting public prophecies by preachers.

— In 1872, as the result of a vast infusion of apparitions and prophecies, Pius IX attempted to quiet them all saying, "A large number of prophecies are in circulation, but I think that they are the fruit of the imagination."

— A number of items in the works of Mary of Agreda, attributed by her to "divine revelation" have been traced back to originating from other books.

— "POEM OF THE MAN GOD" has been condemned, approved, accepted, rejected, verified, and disqualified, seemingly forever.

— Pope Benedict XIII, at the close of the great western schism (1420), was deposed. The story goes that he had relied on a vision from an Abbot who told him what the future would bring. Benedict supposedly based his decisions on this vision and it cost him his position on the pulpit.

The list is much longer. The above material was taken from two books, THE SPIRITUAL LIFE, A Treatise on Mystical Theology by The Very Reverend Adolphe Tanquerey, and from THE GRACES OF INTERIOR PRAYER, A Treatise on Mystical Theology by Rev. A. Poulain, S.J. I do not believe the books are any longer in print. In any case, the above examples show that confusion in matters of private revelation is not limited to just our age. Seems like there were just as many questions throughout the centuries.

Adding to the above examples, "The Life of St. Catherine of Bologna" relates that the devil sometimes appeared to her in the form of the crucified Christ and demanded of her, under the appearance of perfection, the most impossible things in order to drive her to despair.

Benedict XIV came down quite hard on visionaries of his day, stating: "What is to be said of those private revelations which the Apostolic See has approved of, those of the Blessed Hildegard, of St. Bridget and of St. Catherine of Siena? We have already said that those revelations, although approved of, ought not to, and cannot receive from us any assent of Catholic, but only human faith." Well, that may be, but some of the apparitions involving these "saints" were pretty dramatic. In the case of Mary of Agreda, she often times was seen "in levitation." What to make of it all! St. John of the Cross also stated that locutions should be avoided at all costs and no one should seek such things for the devil is looking for that type of soul. Regardless, private revelation is a historical part of our faith and present throughout the Bible.

Some of us might find all of this a little disturbing. But it seems to go with the territory. Thus, the reason for this book. These are very exciting times. Very troubled times, and evidently a time when many people are bringing us some startling news from supernatural visits. It is happening worldwide. With it comes responsibility and a need to discern. There is a possibility that the aspect of discernment has been lacking, so all of these previous pages have been presented to show examples and past experiences of others relating to apparitions, and also the thoughts of some of our past saints. It is all presented not to confuse, but to show a most important need to discern, to sort out. The title of this book is "THOUGHTS." And that is what is being offered—thoughts on the need for discernment and some reasons why it is so important.

So what of all these apparitions, not just in the United States, but throughout the world? Can we state which are authentic? I can't, but we can make an attempt at it through prayer and calling on the Holy Spirit for guidance. It would appear many are true. The fruits are too good and they are apparently standing the test of time (such as Medjugorje). Some are of the devil. Some probably started out true and have been taken over by the wrong spirit. Some are probably the result of well-intentioned souls whose imaginations or powers of discernment have been deluded in the cresendo of supernatural manifestations. Which are which?

Personally, I do not believe there are any private revelations that do not include some area of question and the above examples of some of the difficulties of past saints imply as much. Still, the increase of supernatural manifestations of the past ten years has generated the danger of a new cult whose interest in the latest message of so and so, or the latest prophecy of chastisement is taking precedence over all other matters, including the needs of the Church.

Concerning chastisement, entire volumes are available. But I'm not sure we can give God the blueprint on how all this is going to happen. One point concerns me. It seems that many of the writers of this material today have strong feelings for the events of Medjugorje. But the events of Medjugorje detail ten secrets each visionary is to receive prior to any of this happening. Four of them haven't even received a tenth secret yet. The same was true at Garabandal where a great sign was to occur prior. What has happened to these predictions? Weren't these things supposed to happen before any chastisement was to come?

Many of the excerpts from reported messages shown in this book come from American messengers. They were used simply because more people in this country would be familiar with them. Questions of discernment are a prerequisite with all private revelation and there is no visionary in the world exempt from it. There are still questions regarding some of the events of Medjugorje. This is also true of Christine Gallagher, Pachi Talbott, Maria Esperanza and Josyp Terelya. Vassula Ryden has found many critics.

There is a new book available concerning the incredible story of Julia Kim (Korea). These events come steeped with witnesses, documentation, and undeniable phenomena publicly witnessed by many. Yet the story of Julia's suffering is disturbing, at times grotesque. Mirna (Damascus) fits the same mold, with much credibility, but her situation seems to be caught up by outside influences in a dubious promotional effort. Can any question automatically disqualify any of them? Personally, I don't think so, but that does not eliminate the need to question.

During the last Christmas season, during the first week of advent, the parish we attend had a week of perpetual adoration. I took the hour of three to four in the morning to help fill out the schedule. I had decided to spend the time in meditation and to try to get in touch with the Lord regarding a number of decisions facing our ministry, including the need, or not, of this book. I prayed no rosary, no chaplet, no litany, no formal prayer. Not even one Our Father or Hail Mary. It was an attempt to turn all of my needs over to the Lord and to try to ascertain His will. The hours went quickly and there was no doubt in my mind that indeed, the Lord did speak to me. I left the church after those hours assured of that. I also left the church assured of one other thing. The experience did not make me a locutionist.

Have you ever attended a spiritual retreat or one of those weekends where they go through a special session of trying to truly get in contact with a visible God? We are asked to close our eyes and concentrate very deeply on the image of Jesus—on how we see him—on how we picture Jesus. Some pretty specific images are created, but I can assure you of one thing—that does not make you a visionary. Am I implying that some visionaries are experiencing nothing more than that. No, I don't think so. I don't believe that kind of experience would prompt anyone to write a book about it. But it is important to reflect on from the standpoint of our involvement.

THE RESULTS?

In suggesting the need for discernment, one of the more questionable words I see is "unity." It always seems so right, so Scriptural, so necessary. But perhaps we need to question, "Unity to who?" and "Unity of what?" A visionary in Australia claims a message "demanding" unity of all visionaries. Interestingly, he claims to have been chosen to lead them all. A somewhat similar message was received by a visionary in the United States and called for the joining of all Marian organizations—again under the direction of the visionary involved. This series of messages even included special insight as to who should or should not be admitted to a certain community. Unity, as being presented in the book, "MIRACLE OF DAMASCUS," is apparently only possible if the Pope steps down to allow all churches to come together (Oh boy!).

The watered down faith and borderline ecuminism

which surfaced after Vatican II has obviously brought much confusion in the Church, but I personally do not believe the Church can ever be the stumbling block for the "that all might be one" called for by Jesus Christ. I believe that must happen within Christ's Church, not outside of it.

We can all be assured that the Blessed Virgin Mary does not need my approval for her plans of trying to return all children to her Son. However, looking at the experiences of the past ten years or so, it seems she is very content in doing it on a one person at a time basis. Her messages and appearances come to many, all over the world. She seems to be asking for involvement on a localized or regional basis, not in trying to bring forth a "new messiah." Hence the incredible growth in prayer groups all over the world, the great rush of new Marian Centers and new Marian ministries, the involvement of countless people in her army, are all examples that she steers them all back to the "One Messiah." We are all called.

We may be at the point where we need to further discern the true meaning for this unity and just who we are going to be united to. There is one other spirit that would also like to see total unity, but not for the same reason. In the appendix of this book I am including some rules of discernment. They come from St. Ignatius and from the two books referenced above.

I also believe there is a much stronger need to pray for claimed visionaries than there is a need to go chasing after them. If their experiences are true, then there is a great need for support. It appears there is little spiritual guidance available to them. On the one hand, the Church, overly cautious, provides little direction.

Many priests today are automatically turned off by any such spiritual activity, particularly if it involves Our Lady. On the other hand, priests active in the Marian movement often become too over-zealous in the promotion, and discern nothing. It wouldn't hurt for groups to gather to pray for visionaries instead of just gathering to listen to them, or to just fax their messages around the country. I wonder if discernment might indicate we would be better off without faxing messages? Many have proven to be wrong, misquoted, altered or over-emphasized. I wonder if that is what Our Lady had in mind when she says "Spread my messages." First, she asked us to live them.

At this point, it might be fair for you to ask the question: "Hey, who is this guy giving all this advice on discernment. What authority does he have?" It's a fair question and the answer is I don't have any authority, only concern. In our own ministry we have the same difficulties and discernment needs, and constantly are groping with that problem: should this book be published or shouldn't it? Should this be mentioned or not? When you dedicate your life and your work to Our Lady, she keeps you very busy. And, she has certainly blessed our efforts. Unfortunately, she has not seen fit to give us all the answers beforehand. We struggle to blend our efforts into the existing teachings of the Church.

But even with all of our experiences of the past six years, do I have doubts about some of the Medjugorje messages? Yes I do. How about Vassula, Christine Gallagher? Yes I do. What about Korea, Kibeho, or Josyp Terelya? Absolutely. What about Scottsdale and the I AM YOUR JESUS OF MERCY books? Yes! We may not ever experience an apparition site or a visionary that is without some question. It was there with Bernadette, and it took the Church 14 years to approve of Fatima—in spite of the miracle of the sun. The process of our publishing the Scottsdale books, as well as the book, APOSTOLATE OF HOLY MOTHERHOOD, for example, included some heavy discernment. It involved months, not days. The process did not eliminate every question. Perhaps some will always exist. Not having all the answers seems to force you to rely on the "response of the faithful" as a further means of discernment. What is the response to the book? Through God's grace, undoubtedly, the response to the above books has been incredible. In our case a further measuring stick is the belief that the book should be made available without the thought of profit, and that somehow Our Lady will make it all work economically. It has. So, we don't have all the answers. We struggle the same as you do, trying to align our wills to that of a sometimes mysterious God. Many weeks of study and prayer go into the effort.

It is interesting to note that of the dozens of requests we have received to publish message type books, almost all stressed "extreme urgency" and the specific request of the Blessed Virgin Mary that we publish it. Some came with a specific message for the foundation, and one refused manuscript resulted in our getting a message back (from Our Lady) that was threatening, intimidating, and told me I now had blood on my hands because of my refusal. I really don't think so.

Yes, we have our discernment needs and it seems a constant process for us. I do not know if we have always been right, or that we haven't unintentionally hurt someone along the way through our decisions. But I do know that the foundation has been incredibly blessed, and that our work often times seems to be literally out of our hands. I do not have any visions or receive locutions but I feel one very important Person is pleased with what we do, as well as His Mother. Ultimately, They are the only two I am concerned about pleasing. I am sure all those involved in this great new Marian Movement also feel the same way.

We also feel that our not publishing certain books seemed to have positive results and I have to believe the Lord planned it that way. Where we didn't publish certain books we wound up assisting those involved with help in "how to do it" and put others into business in Our Lady's ministry. It truly appears that Our Lady has preferred to form a network of many individuals, organizations and ministries, all apparently responsible for some aspect of her work.

Being a visionary is not something I wish to be. It would seem the responsibilities and pressures are enormous, not to mention the attacks that most certainly must go with it. On the contrary, I feel very blessed that I can participate in some way through the work of the foundation. That is enough—in fact, it is more than enough. And it does not include being the Lord's watchdog for apparitions or visionaries, or pronouncing judgments regarding them. Perhaps it does include trying to be of assistance in the discernment process of these events and hopefully this book can at least put some questions in the minds of many readers that can be beneficial in their evaluations.

If you study some of the discernment guidelines listed in the appendix of this book, please keep in mind that much of what is shown there was written prior to the events at Fatima in 1917, and the subsequent

crescendo of apparitions since that time. Our Lord and
Our Lady may have proved some of the old theories
obsolete in the process. The appendix also includes
some specific information regarding the thrust of "new
age" infiltration into the Marian movement.

PART III

THE CHURCH

As we would expect, much of the prophecy of the past twenty years involves the Church and Pope John Paul II. During the past several years, he was supposed to have been either assassinated or forced to flee Rome a half-dozen times. Sadly, this is one prophecy we may well yet have to face. Still, the condition of the Church today seemingly warrants any and all such prophecy. The signs of dissent and chaos are everywhere, and the bishops around the world, and particularly in the west, have done little to absolve their lack of responsibility.

Today we have a right-wing and a left-wing, liberals and conservatives, feminist and gay rights groups, pro-abortion groups, dissident theologians and bishops, and a theology that places social justice and environmental concerns ahead of the Blessed Sacrament, the Blessed Virgin Mary, and the elimination of sin. And we wonder why all of this isn't working out better!

What has happened? And what is the solution? Our Lady can only seem to come up with one solution— "Return to My Son." Wow! Could that really be the answer? So simple!

Let's just assume for a moment that it is. In that case, what are we returning from? How about returning from the misinterpretations of Vatican II? That always provokes a lot of pro and con arguments. How about skipping the arguments and just look at the track record since we now have almost 30 years of history to gauge the results. What are they?

— The number of priests, brothers and religious has dropped by 50%, over 200,000 vocations have been lost and the count is rising.

— Mass attendance dropped dramatically. In some countries it is now almost non-existent.

— Seminaries and convents have closed everywhere, and many of those still left teach a theology that a Catholic cannot recognize.

— Churches have been stripped to conform with other faiths under some strange entity called "ecumenism."

— Priests and religious were indoctrinated with the works of para-psychology, social justice, all kinds of equal rights issues, and were left with a hollow shell regarding the once proud tenets of their faith and vocation.

— The sacrament of Confession all but disappeared and with it, not surprisingly, sin as well. Doesn't sin exist anymore?

— Doctrines of the faith fell under the interpretation of any modern day theologian who came along and "The True Presence," Heaven, Hell and Purgatory, the existence of Satan, and allegiance to the Magisterium are seriously questioned.

— New Age philosophies are now a part of many religious orders and have crept into the parishes themselves.

— Catholic schools provide a watered down replica of religious education. In some cases, it is not even recognized as Catholic.

— Some priests and religious became more aware of their lifestyles and the promotion of every cause that came along.

— The Blessed Virgin Mary got dumped into the closet—not too far from the new location of her Son—and many remnants of past Catholicism became the point of scrutiny or abandonment.

— The Mass at times, evolved into a new need to entertain those in attendance rather than a period of worship, and we wonder why so many don't see a need to attend any longer.

— Radical feminist groups, along with gay rights groups and pro-abortion advocates solicited and obtained support from bishops.

— These same Bishops Conferences started to pump out all kinds of social, economic and political pastorals, at the neglect of the spiritual needs of their flock.

— Pre-Vatican II supporters received ridicule while pro-Vatican II advocates jumped off into all sorts of new ideas and ventures, leaving the Church groping somewhere in the middle.

— Open rebellion to the office of the Pope is now common.

— The Bible has become "reinterpreted" over and over. Someone thought Vatican II mandated "liturgical reform," and abuses became commonplace in the Mass, while many other devotions got trashed totally.

— Gays and abortion activists pop up in vocations everywhere, and the number of sex offenses involving the clergy has rocked the Church.

— Some American Bishops, at the promotion of theologians and activist groups, stand poised to invent "The American Catholic Church."

— And, finally, the great apostasy looms on the horizon, ready to fall on all of us.

Is the above litany an accurate reflection of the Church today? Or is it an exaggeration of current trends? After all, there are some very neat things happening in the Church today and not many of us would want to go completely back to the days of old. Well then, what is happening? Let's address that by using two more questions:

1) If there are problems in the Church, can anyone blame them on the decisions reached at Vatican II?

2) And what has all of that to do with the topic of apparitions?

In addressing the first question, it seems like secular humanism, communism, modernism, and all those "isms" have been around for quite awhile. Perhaps Vatican II simply became the vehicle by which they were sort of all issued in. The council certainly wasn't convened with the thought of creating havoc for the Church.

And is the current plight of the Church intimately connected with the surge of apparitions during this same period? It sure seems so, and further, it seems like it has been for the past two centuries. In his book, THE FINAL HOUR, author Michael Brown presents some very convincing evidence that the problems within the Church of today were foretold many, many decades ago. And in more recent times, claimed apparitions at Garabandal, Spain, in the early 1960s provided us with some rather pointed messages regarding the ordained Church. Now that many of those prophecies are being realized, the Church is taking a new look at the Garabandal events. Similar warnings have come on a pretty consistent basis since then, from a number of visionaries. And what of the messages of Fr. Gobbi over the past two decades that seem to be so relevant to what is happening today? There is most certainly an urgent need to discern this crescendo of apparitions and messages, but in the process, there is also a responsibility to recognize that what is happening in the Church today should come as no surprise to us. It is pretty much agreed that the third secret of Fatima, which was not revealed in 1960 as expected, also detailed the future difficulties of the Church.

And so it appears that there is a lot of merit in the words of past and some present visionaries who speak of the plight of Our Lord's Church and His shepherds. We appear to be living the events foretold.

Interestingly, the more you study the documents of Vatican II and the interpretations of many, many writers who evaluate it, you come to recognize the positive potential of the Council and that none of the above items were supposed to happen. Then what did happen? It seems like what did happen was somebody named Satan—ya know, the one who doesn't exist. Pope John XXIII opened a window to let in a breath of fresh air, and guess who came in with it! And he usually comes as an angel of light.

A few weeks ago I read an article by Fr. Robert Fox in a magazine he publishes, where he praised the ecumenism of Vatican II and the great call for unity that it created. That's a rather strange switch. Evidently Pope Paul VI didn't share that same view. In 1965 he stated, "The smoke of Satan has entered the very chimney of the Church," and further, "We have now gone from self-criticism to self-destruction." Whose fault was it? Pope John XXIII gets criticized by many for it, but in his book, THE JOURNEY OF A SOUL, he stated:

> "Jesus, my beloved Lord, has deigned to give me an ever clearer understanding of the necessity of keeping whole and intact my sense of faith and my being of the mind of the Church, and avoiding the so-called Modernist errors, which in a crafty and tempting way are trying to undermine the foundations of Catholic doctrine...The wind of modernism blows very strongly and more widely than seems at first sight, and may very likely strike and bewilder even those who were at first moved only by the desire to adapt the ancient truth of Christianity to modern needs. Many, some of them good men, have fallen into error, perhaps unconsciously; they have let themselves be swept into the field of error."

And so they have. Regardless, the end result is that the 25 years since Vatican II has been one of the greater disasters the Church has seen in two centuries. Yet, even to those who would agree with that statement, there still have been some good fruits produced by the efforts of the Council. It appears that all of that is now past history. Since we have to live in the world of today, and since this is the only world we have to live in, the question is, "What can be done about it?"

If I had to express an opinion, I would say we all have to do two things. First, we have to pray very hard, and very often. Second, it is probably time to stand up for our faith. Material is popping up everywhere exposing some of the things that are going on in the ordained Church, particularly in the schools, convents and seminaries. We have all been witness to some of the same right in our own parishes. There is no possible way I can detail much of it in this book. That will have to wait for a separate book. One senses the revolt may be on. The conference of American bishops stands in the forefront, quietly moving further and further away from the Magisterium and closer and closer to the split. The voices of the dissidents bend their ears while the faithful majority sit silently. I cannot document all of these things from other dioceses, but I could give a pretty good representation of my own diocese (Cincinnati). Many would not believe it. I am not sure very many people even are aware of the changes being made to the Bible, inclusive language, liturgical additions and deletions. Much of this comes from an organization known as ICEL (International Commission for English in the Liturgy). Archbishop Pilarczyk of Cincinnati presides as chairman. And what about the textbooks your children are now using in supposedly Catholic schools. I remember a statement made by the great Bishop Fulton Sheen. He said, "Today, I tell my Catholic friends and relatives to send their children to public colleges where they at least have a chance to fight for their faith, instead of to Catholic ones where it is systematically stripped away from them."

Are you truly aware of what your children are being taught in supposedly Catholic schools? Have you checked their textbooks or questioned the school? You should. Never let any DRE tell you that Vatican II mandated these teachings. That is pure poppycock.

Do you truly believe that if enough people listen to the media and think that birth control and contraception is OK, that it is a personal choice, that can somehow invalidate the teachings of the Pope? Do you believe that any priest or theologian can absolve your responsibilities by merely telling you, "Your own conscience is the rule. If you believe it is right for you then it is OK?" You discern. But if my own privatized conscience is all I need for salvation, then why did Jesus Christ bother to come? If He came to save me from my sins, why did He bother if sin doesn't really exist except in someone's mind? Gee, I thought it said in the "Big Book" that He "came to call sinners, not the self-righteous" and to tell us what is sin and what isn't. Didn't He also say that He would "send the Paraclete" to tell us the truth because our own conscience isn't enough? Did God really call Moses to the mountain to tell him: "Hey, look, I've got a list of ten suggestions here. Why don't you pass these out to the folks and suggest they try to pick out three or four that each feels comfortable with?" I thought they were "commandments," and that you got the whole package—whether you like it or whether you don't.

Our consciences are formed by sound instruction, based on Church Doctrine and Church Tradition. That foundation is vital. If it is absent, anyone is given free reign to form the conscience. Jesus Christ came and set the standard for correct formation of conscience, and He entrusted that standard to the care, nurturing and dissemination of the Roman Catholic Church.

However, if the bishops whose responsibility it is to disseminate the information contained therein choose to fall short of our Holy Father's expectations, the needed guidance is lacking. The bishops' conferences, in oiling the squeakiest wheels and handling the dissident special interest groups with kid gloves, squelch the Church's teaching, as if the Church should be run as a democracy. Priests are silent, for all intents and purposes, at the pulpit. The people crave direction, but what they get is coddling.

To all the faithful bishops in this country, those aligned with the Magisterium, who vocally stand up to abortion, gay rights groups and radical feminist attacks, those who cherish the Mass and the Blessed Sacrament, I believe we owe unwavering support. On an even closer level, I believe we have an obligation to publicly acclaim the efforts of those priests, who at the parish level, profess the same ideals. We cannot give too much time to their needs or to assist in their efforts, and most certainly need to be present and in support of their liturgies, prayer groups and other activities. Most importantly, they need to hear it from each of us. And of course there is a very strong responsibility for prayer for those who seem to fall outside such guidelines.

I do not wish to sound like a revolutionary or add to the trauma. I have enough trouble just trying to save my own soul. At times, I feel I am losing. So there is no sense thinking I can save everyone else's. But we may be at that time where it is going to be necessary to make sure our voices are heard by the bishops involved. Isn't that what the theologians and radical feminist movements have done? The book, CODE OF CANON LAW, is available to anyone. So are all the documents of Vatican II. If you study them, you may come to the opinion that they must be talking about a different church. The Code of Canon Law indicates you not only have a right to speak out for your faith, but an obligation to do so. It also specifically states what the responsibilities of bishops are, not just their authority. Canon law also applies to your rights and duties. The documents of Vatican II outline many of these same points. Some interesting excerpts from the Code of Canon Law:

> Canon #209: "The Christian faithful are bound by an obligation, even in their own patterns of activity, always to maintain communion with the Church."

> Canon #212 includes the statement: "In accord with the knowledge, competence and preeminence which they possess, the Christian faithful have the right and even at times a duty to manifest to the sacred pastors their opinion on matters which pertain to the good of the Church..."

> Canon #213: "The Christian faithful have the right to receive assistance from the sacred pastors out of the spiritual goods of the Church, especially the word of God and the sacraments."

> Canon #217: "The Christian faithful, since they are called by Baptism to lead a life in conformity with the teaching of the Gospel, have the right to a Christian education..."

> Canon #226: "Parents have a most serious obligation and enjoy the right to educate their

children; therefore Christian parents are especially to care for the Christian education of their children according to the teaching handed on by the Church."

Canon #229: "Laypersons are bound by the obligation and possess the right to acquire a knowledge of Christian doctrine adapted to their capacity and condition so that they can live in accord with that doctrine, announce it, defend it when necessary, and be enabled to assume their role in exercising the apostolate." That all sounds pretty specific.

What about the ordained Church, and specifically the bishops and theologians? Some quick references:

Canon #750: "All that is contained in the written word of God or in tradition, that is, in the one deposit of faith entrusted to the Church and also proposed as divinely revealed either by the solemn magisterium of the Church or by its ordinary and universal magisterium, must be believed with divine and Catholic faith. It is manifested by the common adherence of the Christian faithful under the leadership of the sacred magisterium; therefore, all are bound to avoid any doctrines whatever which are contrary to these truths."

Canon #751: "Heresy is the obstinate postbaptismal denial of some truth which must be believed with divine and Catholic faith, or it is likewise an obstinate doubt concerning the same. Apostasy is the total repudiation of the Christian faith. Schism is the refusal of submission to the Roman Pontiff or of commu-

nion with the members of the Church subject
to him."

Canon #380 (for bishops): "Before he takes
canonical possession of his office, the person
promoted is to make a profession of faith and
take an oath of fidelity to the Apostolic See
in accord with a formula approved by the
same Apostolic See..."

Canon #803-2: "It is necessary that the formation and education given in a Catholic
school be based upon the principles of Catholic doctrine; teachers are to be outstanding for
their correct doctrine."

Canon #805: "For his own diocese the local
ordinary has the right to name or approve
teachers of religion and likewise to remove or
to demand that they be removed if it is
required for reasons of religion or morals."

Have you been getting shortchanged here? You discern. I feel confident of one thing: no theologian, himself, has the authority to create, alter, or eliminate any
Catholic doctrine any more than I do, and I have none
at all. It is also quite evident that no Catholic is obliged
to follow any bishop that is not in conformity to the
Magisterium of the Church, and has the right (and
maybe even the obligation) to tell him so.

Most of us grew up under the unwritten law that we
should never criticize a priest—pray for him. Most of
us still adhere to that, but what do we do in our current
situation where we see our faith slowly being stripped
away? Is this just another example of the case where
the squeaky wheel gets the oil—the squeaky wheel
being the theologians and dissidents—while the silent
faithful are left pondering what their faith really

teaches them? You decide. Do certain bishops (Hunt-hausen and Weakland, for example) have the right and authority to teach what they are teaching? It wouldn't seem so. How long should the bishops put up with Greeley, McBrien, Curran, McCormick, Ruether and the new raft of female theologians preaching "Women Church"? Have you seen the new Bible? The new "contemporary English version"? You should. It comes complete with an "Imprimatur." Let's hold all of that for another book.

I wonder also, whether this great shortage of priests and nuns is truly as bad as is claimed, or is some of it self-induced? The answer appears obvious when you suddenly discover that many vocations are pushed away because they are too Catholic, or devoted to Mary, or too "pre-Vatican II."

If you truly believe that a chastisement is in the offing, what specifically do you think will bring it about? It sort of seems like the world needs to first make all the wrong decisions to bring about God's wrath. It's like you can't get a whipping for just thinking about snatching those cookies, you first have to get caught with your hand in the cookie jar. Has the world, and the Church, made all of those choices yet that will require God's intervention? It seems pretty clear that we have made most of them already. And the recent presidential election which appears to have truly endorsed abortion and gay rights just about seals it. What is left to decide? I agree—the Church. Many prophecies today stress the urgency of this current situation.

All of those "in the know," talk of the impending split and the creation of the "American Catholic Church." With it will come, supposedly, married clergy, women priests, gay rights, abortion rights, and "freedom" from Rome. Will that happen? I don't know—(the bishops have not consulted with me yet). But speaking just for myself, I wouldn't mind having it happen tomorrow morning at eight o'clock. At least then we will know why a chastisement is due, and we will then be free to align ourselves with the Roman Catholic Church and know what doctrines we are subscribing to. Sort of sounds like it might be easier.

An alternative? How about suddenly witnessing God's great love, mercy and grace, and see the whole thing come back together? Can He do that, and what will it take? Big order. Our Lady keeps popping up saying that prayer can accomplish everything—if everybody gets involved; and we keep getting these messages about how to accomplish it. But remember, Satan does exist (Our Lord said so), and he is in there to mess it all up wherever possible. Aside from the impending need to stand up for our faith, we still have that need to generate mountains of prayer for the ordained Church. The problems they face in trying to cope with this miserable world are much more difficult than we probably perceive. A strong voice might help, but only if it is backed up by even stronger prayer.

Is there anything else you can do if you feel like you are out in the cold somewhere? It would seem like the first need would be to become involved with a group or organization that has the same concerns. That single voice doesn't seem to generate much response. That might be especially true involving the Catholic education issue, or lack of it. There is a great need for parents to find out what their children are being taught, and to be involved as a body. It may also be worthwhile to become more knowledgeable in regard to the documents of Vatican II and the Code of Canon Law. Work, as an organization, with a priest who also shares your concern, and have him further explain and identify those documents that can verify your needs. Become aware of similar such groups or organizations in your area and unite in a common goal. And finally, at that point take those concerns to your chancery.

I might finish by suggesting some reading material that is available regarding the Church. You certainly need something besides what this writer has to offer. There is plenty available. A number of books worth acquiring, among others, are UNICORN IN THE SANCTUARY, DEFENDING THE PAPACY, and THE CRISIS OF DISSENT from Christendom Publications, and UNGODLY RAGE (radical feminism) from Ignatius Press. THE CATHOLIC ANSWER and CATHOLIC HERITAGE are two excellent magazines dealing with Catholic faith, available from Our Sunday Visitor Press.

There are many newspapers and periodicals available. The liberal and left-wing crowd read the NATIONAL CATHOLIC REPORTER and COMMENWEAL. The conservatives read THE WANDERER. For the majority in the middle, I would suggest the CATHOLIC REGISTER and TWIN CIRCLE. A good periodical magazine is HOMILETIC & PASTORAL REVIEW, 86 Riverside Dr. New York, 10024 ($24.00 per year). The INSTITUTE ON RELIGIOUS LIFE produces a periodical (10 times per year) that is most excellent. Although this publication is principally geared for the religious, it is very Catholic, very faithful to the Church and the Pope, and very informative as to some of the things that are happening in the Church. Send them a donation of $10.00 for a subscription, and probably another $10.00 in donation for some back issues. The address is P.O. Box 41007, Chicago, IL 60641.

There is also a new organization of priests known as CREDO. They exist to battle some of the changes that are being proposed by certain elements regarding a further watering down of the liturgy, inclusive language, etc. They need your donations and your involvement. Address: P.O. Box 7004, Arlington, VA 22207. Find out what is available.

"New age religion" has found its way into the Catholic Church. Do you know what "Creation Spirituality" and "The Enneagram" teach? Two recommended books on current issues are: CATHOLICS AND THE NEW AGE, by Fr. Mitch Pacwa, and WHAT CATHOLICS REALLY BELIEVE, by Karl Keating. These are excellent books, both published by Servant Publications in Ann Arbor, Michigan. The documents of Vatican II can be acquired from: The Daughters of St. Paul, 50 St. Paul Ave., Boston, MA 02130 (ask for their catalog), or from Catholic Book Publishing Co. of New York.

An article published by the Riehle Foundation, titled "The Blessed Virgin Mary and the New Age," has been added to the appendix of this book. Please read it.

I believe Jesus Christ founded one Church. And He said it will always be there, no matter what. The other 350 or 400, mankind founded. Are we about to do it again? You discern.

PART IV

CONCLUSION

We live in extraordinary times. It is absolutely undeniable that there is great dissension in the Church, that the world speeds headlong toward self-destruction and chastisement, and that apparitions and messages are being received everywhere warning us of these things, and how to prevent them.

But there is also a strong need to recognize the fact that neither Our Lady nor we individually are doing battle only with ourselves. There is an opposition in existence, and he is very real, a false angel of light. The battle between the Lady Clothed with the Sun and the red dragon is on folks. Spiritual warfare exists. It has become all too obvious—in our lives, in the media, in society, in governments, even in the Church. It is happening now.

Have we reached the point where we are going to have to truly stand up for our faith? Is the Lord's chastisement looming on the horizon? Is the Church in America truly going to split? Is Satan actively seeking to discredit and destroy all these heavenly visits that seem to be manifesting themselves to so many from Our Lord and Our Lady? Those are the questions before us. For my part, I say "yes" to all of the above.

This book, THOUGHTS, merely tries to identify the need for discernment and provide a few suggestions.

With God all things are possible. The massive problems of the world and the Church require but a simple nod of His head for resolution. Jesus Christ told us that emphatically—that only He can give true peace. I guess then, that Our Lady's recommendations, "Pray, pray, pray," pretty much says it all. That prayer must be for every visionary in the world, for guidance and direction. It must be for every bishop and priest, and brother, and nun, especially for those who have so much difficulty with their vocation and who are being deluded by that evil spirit, the father of all lies and delusion. There is a need to seek God's mercy and it appears we need to be more visible in our efforts— through the sacraments, group prayer, rosaries, adoration of the Blessed Sacrament and allegiance to the Magisterium of the Church. Our faith tells us we already have everything we need to accomplish it; it's all there, in that book called the Bible. We need to recognize God's will and realize that only He is in control. We need to return Jesus Christ to the place of first priority in our lives.

At the same time, we need to be present, and vocal and visible in our faith. If that is not a requirement then why did Our Lord bother to send the Holy Spirit to empower the Apostles, to send them out to preach, and to build the body of the Church? And in our daily lives, and in our day to day activities of trying to seek out the Lord and in trying to respond to the requests of His Mother, we need to discern.

There may be a much greater need to pray for visionaries and special messengers than there is to go chasing after them. "Living the messages" may not entail visiting every apparition site that comes along, or accepting every message on face value alone. The color of your rosary is not as important as whether you pray with it, and the recognition that Christ physically comes to us every day in every Mass is more important than any sign in the sky. We need to attempt to discern everything, not only from a visionary but even within the ordained Church concerning some of those teachings that raise doubt or strong concern in our minds. We need to make that commitment to Christ, His Mother, and His Church and Vicar, and then to replace fear with hope. Maybe we need to worry less about our physical chastisement and more about the state of our souls, and how we get to where HE is.

I wonder if God sees more value in our taking fifteen minutes to quietly talk with Him than in spending hours listening to someone speak about Him? Is there more value praying a rosary at an apparition site, or in front of an abortion clinic? I don't know. Should you simply pray for a bishop who doubts the Pontiff, and say nothing, or should you attempt to defend the beliefs of your faith? How about doing both? How about praying a rosary at an apparition site and at an abortion clinic. We all need to be involved, and we all need to recognize the value of that word "conversion." From all of Our Lady's messages, and right through the words of the Gospels, that seems to be where it is all at. And it seems to be directed to each of us individually.

Since many are returning to the Sacraments of the Church through apparition messages, it is rather ridiculous today to doubt the existence of apparitions occurring throughout the world. There are too many, too many good fruits, and too many identical messages. I also truly believe they are also occurring in the United States. But, Satan is obviously present and bent on confusing and destroying. He is misguiding us.

"Unity?" I wonder if you can ever achieve it with the Orthodox Churches if you can't achieve it within the Roman Catholic Church?

There also seems little doubt that the ordained Church bears some of the responsibility for this sudden surge by so many toward claimed apparitions and messages. If spiritual needs are not being met from the pulpit, people will go somewhere else where they will be. If devotion to the Blessed Virgin Mary, adoration of the Blessed Sacrament, the need for the sacrament of Confession, participation in the rosary, promotion of prayer groups, commitment to the Magisterium of the Church, and spiritual direction and guidance are not being made available in the parish today, then you cannot fault the laity for seeking these basic tenets of our faith from other sources.

Fortunately, I can attest to the fact that that is just not me talking. When you receive between 100 and 200 letters and phone calls a day, every day, for a number of years, you get a pretty good feel for what the people are saying and experiencing all across the country. And what they are experiencing is neglect, and watered down Catholicism, or worse.

The rest of the bad news is that Satan can have a field day in that type of situation. And he apparently is. Evidently Lucifer can and does come as an "angel of light" and can draw many people into following apparently good messages with the intent of blowing the whole thing up somewhere down the road. "He's meaner than a junk yard dog," as the saying goes.

Whether you receive material from the Riehle Foundation, or from anywhere else, discern everything. If you are comfortable with it, if it brings you peace and directs you back to the sacraments, if it increases your faith, hang on to it. If it brings you turmoil, doubt, or an uneasy feeling, drop it.

In attempting to weed through this process of conversion and discernment and salvation, it was evidently all so simple to Jesus that He needed only three lines to cover it all. He spelled it out in His very first public message:

> *This is the time of fulfillment. The reign of God is at hand! Reform your lives, and believe in the Gospel!* (*Mark* 1:15).

Maybe it is no more complicated than that.

APPENDIX I

PRIVATE REVELATIONS
Suggested Rules for Discernment

It should be noted that the following criteria was taken from Mystical Theology Treatises which have been in the Church for many years. It would seem that the explosion of apparitions in this century, and the position of the current Church with respect to private revelation, might indicate a need to further define or alter some of these suggested principles of the earlier Church. The following material was taken from: THE SPIRITUAL LIFE by Adolphe Tanquerey S.S., D.D., and THE GRACES OF INTERIOR PRAYER by A. Poulain, S.J.

THE MANNER IN WHICH REVELATIONS ARE MADE

1) Visions (Apparitions);

2) Supernatural Words (Locutions);

3) Divine Touches (Charisms);

VISIONS are supernatural perceptions of some object naturally invisible to man. They are of three kinds:

a) Sensible or corporeal: where the senses actually perceive;

b) Imaginative: produced in the imagination by the supernatural, either during sleep or while awake;

c) Intellectual visions: where the mind perceives a spiritual truth without the aid of the senses.

SUPERNATURAL WORDS are manifestations of divine thought conveyed to the exterior or to the interior senses, or directly to the intelligence.

DIVINE TOUCHES are spiritual sentiments of goodness impressed upon the will.

RULES FOR THE DISCERNMENT OF REVELATIONS

Concerning the subject and object of the revelation:

1) Is the person well-balanced or affected by hysteria or emotional outbursts?

2) Is the person in possession of common sense and sound judgment, as opposed to a vivid imagination?

3) Is the person thoroughly sincere as opposed to having the habit of exaggerating?

4) Does the person have solid and tried virtue and a sense of sincere and deep humility?

5) Does the person take the revelation to a spiritual director and follow the lead of the Church?

6) Is the revelation in opposition to any truth of faith?

7) Is it opposed to any moral law?

8) Does it demand the impossible of the seer?

FIVE CAUSES OF POTENTIAL ERROR THAT CAN INFLUENCE PRIVATE REVELATIONS

1) Faulty interpretations of the message or vision by the visionary;

2) Ignorance of the fact that historic events are often given with approximate truth only;

3) The mingling of human activity with supernatural action during the revelation;

4) A subsequent, but involuntary, modification of the message made by the visionary;

5) Embellishments made by secretaries or compilers of the material.

FIVE POTENTIAL CAUSES THAT SHOW A PRIVATE REVELATION IS NOT AUTHENTIC

1) Simulation: Being untruthful as to the event or message;

2) An over-active mind or imagination;

3) The illusion of the memory: leads us to believe in events that never happened;

4) An action by Satan;

5) The inventions of falsifiers: Either by the visionary involved, or by associated individuals who seek some personal, public or political gain, or notoriety connected to the event.

DESCRIPTIVE DETAILS CONCERNING INTERIOR LOCUTIONS

(Words from St. Teresa of Avila)

1) WHEN do they occur? "Often it is outside the ecstasy; and often it is unexpected,

when the mind is occupied with other things."

2) CLEARNESS: "The interior words are very distinctly formed...they are much more clearly understood than they would be if they were heard by the ear in normal conversation."

3) STRENGTH: "There is no escape, for in spite of ourselves, we are compelled to listen. And the understanding must apply itself thoroughly to what God wills we should hear, so that it matters little whether we will it or not."

4) CERTAINTY: "The words, their effects and the assurance they carry convince the soul at that moment that they come from God."

5) What FEELINGS, what emotional states, do these words produce? "There is a great calm and a peaceful recollection which dwells in the soul together with a desire to praise God."

6) MAJESTY: "With divine locution, we listen as we would to a person of great holiness, learning or authority. They make us tremble."

7) KNOWLEDGE: "Divine locutions instruct us without loss of time, and we understand matters which seem to require a month on our part to arrange."

8) EFFECTS: "Does the divine locution counsel or command an interior disposition—such as to bid the soul to be at peace or correct some defect? They produce this change suddenly in the soul."

9) PERSISTENCE in the memory: "A proof is that these words do not pass from the memory, but remain there for a very long time."

Additional note on the above topics:

When judging private revelation, three steps should be followed at the outset: Obtain detailed information regarding the person involved, also as to all the actual facts of the revelation. Lastly, discern a conclusion based on this information. A process of exclusion can also be used. This consists in proving that neither the Devil nor the individual's mind could have added to God's actions, and that no one retouched the revelation afterwards.

NINE POINTS TO CONSIDER IN THE EVALUATION OF PRIVATE REVELATION. (From Rev. A. Poulain, S.J.)

1) Is there authentic text? Has anything been added, corrected or suppressed?

2) Is it in accord with the dogmas and teachings of the Church?

3) Is anything contrary to faith and morals?

4) Is the revelation useful for our eternal salvation?

5) Are the detailed circumstances of the apparition in keeping with the dignity and seriousness of the Divine Majesty?

6) What sentiments of peace, or, on the other hand, of disquiet, does the person experience during the revelation, or afterward?

7) Does the revelation call for some bold enterprise, such as establishing a new devo-

tion, founding a new congregation or religious organization, building a church? Is this enterprise good for the Church?

8) Have the apparitions or messages stood the test of time and scrutiny?

9) What fruits have been produced, and are they beneficial to the Church?

Additional notes on:

False prophets: They do not allow themselves to be easily discouraged by their repeated failures. They always find some good reason to explain them away, or they pretend that the event is only delayed! When necessary, they proceed to confirm their first prophecy by some new revelation.

False locutions: There is a strange confusion between the "imagination," which constructs a scene, and the "memory," which affirms that it took place. Reason no longer distinguishes between these two very different operations.

RULES FOR THE DISCERNMENT OF SPIRITS
(Taken from THE SPIRITUAL EXERCISES OF ST. IGNATIUS)

1) It is characteristic of God and His Angels, when they act upon the soul, to give true happiness and spiritual joy, and to banish all the sadness and disturbances which are caused by the enemy.

It is characteristic of the evil one to fight against such happiness and consolation by proposing fallacious reasonings, subtilties, and continual deceptions.

2) God alone can give consolation to the soul without any previous cause. It belongs

solely to the Creator to come into a soul, to leave it, to act upon it, to draw it wholly to the love of His Divine Majesty. I said without previous cause, that is, without any preceding perception or knowledge of any subject by which a soul might be led to such a consolation through its own acts of intellect and will.

3) If a cause precedes, both the good angel and the evil spirit can give consolation to a soul, but for a quite different purpose. The good angel consoles for the progress of the soul, that it may advance and rise to what is more pefect. The evil spirit consoles for purposes that are the contrary, and that afterwards he might draw the soul to his own perverse intentions and wickedness.

4) It is a mark of the evil spirit to assume the appearance of an angel of light. He begins by suggesting thoughts that are suited to a devout soul, and ends by suggesting his own. For example, he will suggest holy and pious thoughts that are wholly in conformity with the sanctity of the soul. Afterwards, he will endeavor little by little to end by drawing the soul into his hidden snares and evil designs.

5) We must carefully observe the whole course of our thoughts. If the beginning and middle and end of the course of thoughts are wholly good and directed to what is entirely right, it is a sign that they are from the good angel. But the course of thoughts suggested to us may terminate in

something evil, or distracting, or less good than the soul had formerly proposed to do. Again, it may end in what weakens the soul, or disquiets it; or by destroying the peace, tranquillity, and quiet which it had before, it may cause disturbance to the soul. These things are a clear sign that the thoughts are proceeding from the evil spirit, the enemy of our progress and eternal salvation.

6) When the enemy of our human nature has been detected and recognized by the trail of evil marking his course and by the wicked end to which he leads us, it will be profitable for one who has been tempted to review immediately the whole course of the temptation. Let him consider the series of good thoughts, how they arose, how the evil one gradually attempted to make him step down from the state of spiritual delight and joy in which he was, till finally he drew him to his wicked designs. The purpose of this review is that once such an experience has been understood and carefully observed, we may guard ourselves for the future against the customary deceits of the enemy.

7) In souls that are progressing to greater perfection, the action of the good angel is delicate, gentle, delightful. It may be compared to a drop of water penetrating a sponge.

The action of the evil spirit upon such souls is violent, noisy, and disturbing. It may be compared to a drop of water falling upon a stone.

In souls that are going from bad to worse, the action of the spirits mentioned above is just the reverse. The reason for this is to be sought in the opposition or similarity of these souls to the different kinds of spirits. When the disposition is contrary to that of the spirits, they enter with noise and commotion that are easily perceived. When the disposition is similar to that of the spirits, they enter silently, as one coming into his own house when the doors are open.

8) When consolation is without previous cause, as was said, there can be no deception in it, since it can proceed from God our Lord only. But a spiritual person who has received such a consolation must consider it very attentively, and must cautiously distinguish the actual time of the consolation from the period which follows it. At such a time the soul is still fervent and favored with the grace and aftereffects of the consolation which has passed. In this second period the soul frequently forms various resolutions and plans which are not granted directly by God our Lord. They may come from our own reasoning on the relations of our concepts and on the consequences of our judgments, or they may come from the good or evil spirit. Hence, they must be carefully examined before they are given full approval and put into execution.

APPENDIX II

THE BLESSED VIRGIN MARY
and the New Age

The "thoughts" presented in the previous pages of this book have been produced to show:

A need for discernment,

A danger of jeopardizing your faith by relying too much on too many messages of chastisement, and

That Satan is ever present and desirous of deceiving us as that false angel of light.

The discernment process may not seem too complex regarding the claimed seer, "The Little Pebble," who claims messages that he is to unite and direct all of the visionaries of the world; that he has all of the steps and stages of the chastisement and end times; and that he has been chosen to be the next pope. That might also apply to the writings of an author known as "The Publican" who uses 300 plus pages in a book titled, "THE MIRACLE OF DAMASCUS," to lead us to the conclusion that unity of all churches is only possible if the pope steps down. The discernment process can become much more difficult in trying to evaluate the status of many current visionaries and their messages, such as the automatic writing process of Vassula, or of locutionists who at times seem to be able to pull messages from their mind at random.

However, those basically involve individuals. We are all free to believe or not, and not even belief in Fatima and Lourdes is a prerequisite of our faith. There does appear to be a more insidious movement underfoot.

As we desperately struggle to keep up with the most recent avalanche of new apparitions and claimed visionaries, and discern the merits of new books sweeping across America with more heavenly messages, we feel a need to address a very serious problem that is becoming more and more apparent. New Age religious efforts have decided to jump on the "Mother Mary" bandwagon. (That title, "Mother Mary," is your first key to be cautious of what you are reading.)

The first round came from a woman named Corinne Heline, who authored a book titled, "THE LIFE AND MISSION OF THE BLESSED VIRGIN." Corinne Heline claims she covers details in the life of Mary which are not generally known or fully appreciated. Her background would indicate as much: a life-long study of the ancient mysteries and mystics, studying under Max Heindel (Mason and Rosicrucian), providing a seven-volume New Age interpretation of the Bible, and producing such works as "TAROT AND THE BIBLE" and "MYSTIC MASONRY AND THE BIBLE." Another book hit the market titled "FATIMA PROPHECY," authored by Benjamin Krem. It also attempts to incorporate new age principles into Mary's prophecies and messages.

Then two years ago, "MARY'S WAY" came into print. This book is authored by Peggy Tabor Millin and published by a New Age publishing house, Celestial Arts, in Berkeley, California. Peggy Millin does a masterful job at integrating the events of Medjugorje to New Age philosophies. Indeed, she claims Medjugorje changed her life forever (a claim many of us have made). Still, she refers to Medjugorje as a "divine source," in keeping with her studies in metaphysics, attitudinal healing, and Siddha Yoga. Her first difficulty was accepting the recognition of the "Creator" as masculine. She defines the Croatian Mass as "mesmerizing, like a mantra that takes one immediately to that Inner Room." She defines Mary as the "feminine energy that can save the world." She states: "For years, I have judged the statues and rosaries and crucifixes as being 'englightened.' In a flash, I realize that they are really no different from crystals and mandalas and the Sanskrit Om." And so it goes.

However, the most serious manipulation of Mary's appearances come from a book that is now making the rounds under the title, "MARY'S MESSAGE TO THE WORLD." It is authored by Annie Kirkwood from Carrolton, Texas. The book is published by Blue Dolphin Publishing Company in California. Annie Kirkwood states that the messages should be understood not as words spoken directly by Mother Mary, but received in the form of "interior locutions." It is further stated that, for Catholics, the publication is in conformity with the directives published by Pope Paul VI in 1966 regarding apparitions and revelations.

With that said, the book can best be described as a New Age catechism. It is also a masterful blending of Catholic and other Christian truths with New Age beliefs and mysticism. The result is an artful combination of everything anyone would want to hear, as long as you believe that every person is a god and can control all spirit life.

Mrs. Kirkwood, assisted by her husband, Byron, an engineer heavily involved in the earth sciences, gives vivid description of the impending chastisements down to the last detail. This cosmic revolution, however, will be caused by mother earth as a punishment for what mankind has done to her, and not by God.

There are many alleged quotations in "MARY'S MESSAGE TO THE WORLD" which are so bizarre, contrary to traditional belief, and in direct opposition to revealed truth as found in the Bible, as to make knowledgeable people bristle with indignation. There are even alleged quotes by Mary and Jesus which are designed to appear as if they confirm and more fully explain messages emanating from well known apparition sites.

Following are some quotations taken from the book. These are allegedly from Mother Mary directly:

— This is the same message, in book form, that is being received by the children in Yugoslavia, Lubbock, Texas, and others around the world.

— As for the other lives which I and Joseph lived, this is the truth: every person leads one continuous life. It does not matter, as some churches think, if you believe or not. In the early days of the Catholic Church, this teaching was known and believed.

— The planet earth is being bomarded with forces which will cuase it to change its direction in relationship to the universe. . .as the universe and galaxies grow they will divide and split. The earth will turn on its side. UFO activity will increase.

— After the turning of the earth, there will be two suns. This will become a binary solar system.

— In the last years UFOs will be seen almost daily. They will come in great numbers and will try to make your governments on earth understand that they come in peace. On other planets there are already stations which have been prepared and are being stocked for man's arrival for survival.

REVELATION FROM MOTHER MARY ON HER MARRIED LIFE:

— We were instructed in giving Jesus as much schooling as we could. He was sent to a school between Nazareth and Egypt. It was a school which taught the spiritualness of all beings. He was there for two years. At the age of fourteen Jesus was apprenticed to a distant relative in another land. This was our way of keeping Jesus hidden until he was to begin his mission.

— Our first child after Jesus was James. Then David and Daniel were born eleven months apart...Then there was Elizabeth...Next was Jacob...Then came sweet Ruth...Our last child was Mary Martha (8 children).

Mary and Joseph have been together in other lifetimes, according to the author, claiming that Joseph had already been studying in the different temples of knowledge, light and wisdom (in the spiritual realm) when Mary died. Her next lifetime was as a nun in the Middle Ages.

In another life as a nun Mary apparently returned and became one of the followers of Saint Francis of Assisi...In one lifetime, Joseph and Mary returned as nuns together and were close friends in this service, but Joseph did not like life as a female...In another lifetime, Mary returned as a healer in India. The book goes on to state:

— View love and light, in that it is a measure of what can be. Love can be used to travel in record time. You on earth now have a concept of traveling the speed of light. But have you considered the possibility of traveling at the speed of love?...One day you will be able to send your body on the wings of love.

— I wish all people to turn to God and look to their own God-Mind connection to see them through the coming earth changes. The Church is aware of my predictions and still it withholds the information.

— On earth you have been caught up in certain terms which cause you problems. One term is "salvation." What are you being saved from? How are you saved? Certainly not by magic or by passing your body or body parts through water, however it has been blessed. Nor is there any special plan which you must follow...Another term is the "power of the cross." The only power or magic within any of these symbols is the power which comes from your belief and faith.

— Another term which is sometimes confusing to people is "Heaven." Heaven is a state of mind. It is not a location, but a way of viewing events around you. Heaven is wherever you are on the earth plane or in spirit. Also hell...Heaven and hell are simply mental states.

— All this discussion over interpretations of the Bible is futile. All the arguments about which religion is correct are wasted effort. Put aside the explanations of each Bible verse. Go to the altar in your mind. There confess yourself to God. Your connection to God is not strengthened in some building, or by another's blessing you with water, or by performing any ritual over your physical body.

According to the author, life does not begin at birth and end at death. This is a fallacy in the minds of men. This mentality has been called the earth-mind consciousness. Mary explains that we live many lives, one at a time, and, at times two or more at a time. The spirit-you can incarnate into different cultures, different sexes, different parts of the world and we do not have to do or believe anything to have this life. We already have it and already have lived for eons, first in one body, then in another, according to the book.

Annie Kirkwood claims Mary mentions another concept which is accepted in other parts of the world—that of Karma. This is another word for keeping up with all the aspects of your being. This record of your deeds is kept in your book of life. Evidently, there is also a time of rest. After a death, especially after a violent life, there is a period of rest for the soul. These souls remain in a state of suspended animation for many eons...Hitler is one of these souls.

The final chapter of the book includes a message from Jesus, to give credibility to Mary's messages. In this chapter, Jesus states:

— All these messages in this writing is real and is truth.

— All of you have had eternal life...Each of you have lived before. When I said I came to give life, I did not mean that you did not have life, but that you were not appreciating life.

— This is not a new way of communicating with me; it has a new name—"automatic writing." This is the method I used to help the disciples write the story of my life...What today is called "channeling" is not a new way of communicating with God.

(Jesus goes on to explain the meaning of the Book of Revelation. It is an interpretation that will astonish any Scripture scholar. It includes:)

— Now when you read the story of the pregnant woman and the dragon, realize that the woman is Mother Earth. It could be said Mother Earth is pregnant with the child of a new era.

— There is no big devil, except in your thoughts. There is no great war occurring in Heaven, except in the minds of men...You need no longer be afraid of the beast because you recognize that he is an illusion.

The New Age proponents have definitely decided it will be profitable to incorporate Mary and apparitions in their diabolical goals to overthrow Christianity. Along these lines, Annie Kirkwood has now started to distribute a newsletter. Naturally, it is called "Mary's Message/Newsletter," and it cleverly incorporates Mary's believable messages with heretical input as outlined in the above quotations from the book.

Additionally, the newsletter comes with a flyer from B & A Products Company (Byron & Annie), and includes offerings of books ("MARY'S WAY" by Peggy Millin), materials on how to survive the chastisement, and a map of the futuristic United States after it splits in two.

Discern, folks. Do not allow yourself to be duped. This is serious stuff. Perhaps there is a certain evil spirit that has successfully infiltrated the projects of otherwise well-intentioned people. We must be cautious that we do not put ourselves and others in a position of destroying the tremendous spiritual good that abounds in and through Our Lady's true messages. New age is big time, and it is everywhere. It comes in much more subtle form than as shown in the book by Annie Kirkwood. It is disguised and coated. Like that false "angel of light," it usually appears as something for our own good. Be careful, your soul is at stake.

If you do not know the inner workings of "holistic health," "The Enneagram," "Creation Spirituality," "Christ Consciousness," "Jungian Psychology," and dozens of other heavily masked new age concepts, then please consider obtaining the books listed at the end of this appendix. They are recommended, current, and vital.

Mary has become big business, like it or not. The new age movement is fully aware of that. They are also fully aware of the great interest many people are showing in visionaries. As an aid to further identify some of these more masked new age concepts, the following list of buzz words are provided. Please discern.

Words associated with new age concepts:

Christ Consciousness	Cosmic Christ
God Self	Mind dynamics
Feminist spirituality	Value assessment
Centering techniques	Holistic Health
Creation Spirituality	Global consciousness
One world order	Spiritual energy or plane
Mind control	Bio-feedback
Chakras & Mantras	Inter-connectedness
Green movement	Enneagram
Spirit guides	Transcendance
Divine energy	Communion with the
Theosophy	universe
Yoga	Pantheism
Wicca (Witchcraft)	

Suggested book list:

CATHOLICS AND THE NEW AGE by Fr. Mitch Pacwa, S.J. (Servant Publications)

CULTS, SECTS & THE NEW AGE by Fr. James LeBar (Our Sunday Visitor Press)

UNICORN IN THE SANCTUARY by Randy England

INSIDE THE NEW AGE NIGHTMARE by Randall Bear (Huntington House Publ.)

UNGODLY RAGE (radical feminism) by Donna Steichen (Ignatius Press)

WHAT CATHOLICS REALLY BELIEVE by Karl Keating (Servant Publications)

(If you cannot locate the publishers of the above books, contact The Riehle Foundation.)

THE
RIEHLE
FOUNDATION...

The Riehle Foundation is a non-profit, tax-exempt, charitable organization that exists to produce and/or distribute Catholic material to anyone, anywhere.

The Foundation is dedicated to the Mother of God and her role in the salvation of mankind. We believe that this role has not diminished in our time, but, on the contrary has become all the more apparent in this the era of Mary as recognized by Pope John Paul II, whom we strongly support.

During the past five years the foundation has distributed over three million books, films, rosaries, bibles, etc. to individuals, parishes, and organizations all over the world. Additionally, the foundation sends materials to missions and parishes in a dozen foreign countries.

Donations forwarded to The Riehle Foundation for the materials distributed provide our sole support. We appreciate your assistance, and request your prayers.

IN THE SERVICE OF JESUS AND MARY
All for the honor and glory of God!

The Riehle Foundation
P.O. Box 7
Milford, OH 45150

THE RIEHLE FOUNDATION

- Publisher of religious books

- Distributor of Catholic books, Bibles, rosaries and other materials

- Distributes a monthly newsletter

- Distributes materials to prisons, hospitals and schools

- Serves other non-profit organizations with religious materials

- Distributes religious materials to Catholic missions and churches in foreign countries

- Helps send priests and religious on pilgrimages

- Helps outreach ministries

- Promotes devotion and honor to the Mother of God

- Supports allegiance to the Pope and obedience to the precepts established by the Magesterium of the Church